The Stars Deserve A Second Look

Other Available Titles

"An Introduction to the Seven Spirits of God"

"The Spiritual Dynamics of Hand Drumming"

"A Mystical Introduction to Angels"

Second Edition – Feb 2015
Second Print – 23 February 2015
First Edition – Jan 2015
First Print – 16 January 2015

Table of Contents

Preface

According to Wikipedia, man's earliest understandings of the stars were based upon a literal interpretation of verses in the first book of the bible, Genesis. Stars were fixed points of light "stuck" to a black "fabric" called the firmament.

Then one day someone turned their eyes upward and took a long look at the firmament. They started wondering about those lights and the next thing you know a science was formed; the science called astronomy.

The stars twinkled and a new business was birthed from that old science. The stargazers began making star charts and new titles were formed: Astronomers and Astrologers.

With more upward looks, they observed that some of the "fixed lights" were moving. They named these 'wandering stars', planets. (Note: the Greek word for wander is 'planet') Based on that simple definition - all stars are planets since they all move.

Fast forward to magi, poems, songs, planetariums, telescopes, NASA, the Hubble telescope - and the stars have become quite the celebrities.

So are they just high altitude evening entertainment or is there more than meets the eye? This book will attempt to find out if there are more to stars than just their enchanting beauty and horoscopes.

The way to live the BEST life cannot be found on earth.

So the multitude of stars provokes a question, "Who created all the stars?" I believe if you seek the answer; you'll find the answer. I propose that the stars not only proclaim the glory of God but also communicate insights into living the life that was designed for you - before you came to earth.

The stars are just one of many "signs" leading to The Life. The Life (Yeshua) will also point to your future, a vital union with your Heavenly Father.

> ### Isaiah 40:26 (NLT)
> *"Look up into the heavens. Who created all the stars? He brings them out like an army, one after another, calling each by its name. Because of His great power and incomparable strength, not a single one is missing."*

YHVH names each star; names infer purpose. YHVH has a name for you; your name infers your purpose. I believe we need to know our purpose and understand their (stars) purposes. The purposes YHVH designs for all His creations are unique and special. Many of us do not realize our uniqueness and live boring, normal, unfulfilled lives.

Let's decide **NOT** to be NORMAL

This book will attempt to provide a means for you to leave 'the ways of normal' and walk in <u>His ways</u> and purposes.

Introduction

"Twinkle, twinkle, little star,
How I wonder what you are.
Up above the world so high,
Like a diamond in the sky.

Twinkle, twinkle, little star,
How I wonder what you are.
How I wonder what you are."
- Jane Taylor (1806)

Most people when looking up are amazed by the "artwork" of the night skies. Or maybe your awe of the night stems from episodes of "Star Trek", "Star Wars" or "Doctor Who". Possibly you were captivated by a cosmology course in school. In any case, I hope you stay motivated to carry on star gazing.

As a seeker of truth, I hope the reader will not be distracted by the scientific or the religious terms used in this book. Many groups go back and forth on the belief that the universe is expanding, contracting, or neither expanding nor contracting. Based upon the current astronomical observations, the universe is expanding from a point of origin that astrophysicists call "singularity". Scientists continue to look to the stars for answers. According to the last Hubble data, the observable universe is estimated to contain more than 200 billion galaxies.

Genesis 1:14 (NLT)
*"And God saith, `Let luminaries be in the expanse of the heavens, to make a separation between the day and the night, **then they have been for signs**, and for seasons, and for days and years"*

Those lights in the sky are "**signs**" and what are signs for? Every sign has a message that benefits the reader(watcher).

> ### Daniel 12:3,4 (AMP)
> *3And the teachers and those who are wise shall shine like the **brightness of the firmament**, and those who turn many to righteousness (to uprightness and right standing with God) [shall give forth light] like the **stars** forever and ever.*
>
> *4But you, O Daniel, shut up the words and seal the Book until **the time of the end**. [Then] many shall run to and fro and search anxiously [through the Book], and knowledge [of God's purposes as revealed by His prophets] shall be increased and become great.*

The "brightness of the firmament", I assume is a reference to the stars. Wise teachers and His prophets will continue to reveal the knowledge of God's purposes. I believe, this is that day, "the time of the end". The book is open and there is much revelation available to all who will honor, search, and receive. In this day, **the purpose of the "stars" is being revealed!** It is being revealed so we can act, be changed, and reveal His glory.

I also believe, we will see that we function as bridges between the celestial and the terrestrial. It is time, we understand our role with individual stars and groups of stars. We will gain a keener understanding of the role and purposes of the zodiac, also known as the Mazzaroth.

So join me in the heavens and take a second look,

New Mystic

Chapter 1 – Definition

According to the Wiktionary, **stars** are any small luminous dots appearing in the cloudless portion of the night sky, especially with a fixed location relative to other such dots. *(In parts of North America, "dots" are candy.)* The astronomy definition for **stars:** "luminous celestial bodies, made up of plasma (particularly hydrogen and helium) and having a spherical shapes". The book of Genesis defines **stars** as "lights".

According to the bible on the third day of creation, the Creator created these heavenly bodies, stars.

> ### Genesis 1: 14-16
> *¹⁴ And God said, **<u>Let there be lights</u>** in the expanse of the heavens to separate the day from the night, and let them be signs and tokens [of God's provident care], and [to mark] seasons, days, and years*
>
> *¹⁵ And let them be lights in the expanse of the sky to give light upon the earth. And it was so.*
>
> *¹⁶ And God made the two great lights— the greater light (the sun) to rule the day and the lesser light (the moon) to rule the night. **He also made the <u>stars</u>.***

Paleo Hebrew

So let's go a little deeper and explore the Hebrew definition for "star", kokab (כּוֹכָב). According to a bible concordance, the word is used 37 times.

A possible Paleo Hebrew understanding of the word is:

Letter	Symbolic Meaning	Literal Meaning
כ	Arm, wing, open hand	Strength, to cover, allow
ו	Add, secure, hook	Nail
כ	Arm, wing, open hand	Strength, to cover, allow
ב	Household, in, into	Tent, house

A symbolic interpretation: "Covering the house"

The stars were placed in sky to "give light upon the earth"; the stars are covering our home, our house.

A literal interpretation: "A secure covering & strong house"

The stars rule the night. The Creator strategically placed each star as a secure covering. With the covering of the celestial houses, the earth remains secure.

Are the stars covering until we mature and take their place?

The Creator has a purpose, mission, and reason for all that He does. Maybe, we were created to find out what those stars are really doing up there.

'Celestial' Double-Slit Experiment

Is it possible that our "looking up", our observations influence the stars? Could it be that we get to participate in a "celestial double-slit experiment"? In the original energy experiment, scientists watched a small portion of energy pass through two slits in a barrier. The energy behaved like a particle and went through one slit or the other. Yet when the experiment was repeated in the exact same controlled environment without a human watching (interacting) with the energy, it acted like a wave. Instead of selecting one of the two slits the energy went through both slits at the same time. At a minimum, this energy experiment demonstrates that the behavior of energy was changed based on a person's observation (interaction).

With more observation, we may find that we have more power with the stars than we imagine. We are more powerful and influential than we know. When we observe the stars, we may influence their position. When we observe the stars, we may influence their purpose just like when the scientist looked at the particle.

Proverbs 25:2
*"It is the glory of God to conceal a thing,
but the glory of **kings** is to **search** out a
thing."*

So let's take the challenge and search out the purposes of the zodiac. Let's find out if we have a role with the Mazzaroth.

Chapter 2 – The Stargazer

Genesis 5: 22
"Enoch walked with God for 300 years..."

Enoch's three hundred years of interactive friendship began in this realm and then he went full-time into God's domain. When I first read about Enoch, I imagined Enoch walking down a road talking with God. It took him 300 years to convince God to take him off the earth. I believe they may have started with simple conversations but I now believe that once Enoch got to **know God**; together they did great exploits. Friends do things together. Friends learn from each other. Friends make memories. Friends take on each other's qualities.

We should learn all that we can from all the relationships that God has had with different earth dwellers. With that knowledge, we would could establish stronger beliefs and correct expectations about our relationship with Him. God established a precedent with Adam. Adam and God did stuff together in a garden. I'm sure they did more together in the garden than what is documented. Adam did a great job naming the animals. I believe the names he gave provided identity, purpose and worth to the new creations.

I believe our Creator likes to 'co-create' with His friends. I believe it's time to properly use our imagination to have godly fantasies of interaction with the Godhead. I know some of us are still renewing our minds from images of heaven being filled with clouds and fat cherubs playing harps...

Who will be the next friend of God?

There are documents that have captured accounts of Enoch's "extracurricular" activities. I'm betting that some of those activities are equal to or exceed his accolade of being the first documented person to leave earth without dying. According to his book, "The Book of Enoch", he acquired much from his unique relationship with God.

We know that the stars are signs; I believe Enoch learned how to read those signs. The book of Enoch contains a section called "The Heavenly Luminaries". This section of Enoch's book captures celestial observations, star facts, and mentions how to track the movements of the sun and moon. I believe, the Heavenly Tablets were his "Rosetta Stone". There is more detailed on Enoch in Helena Lehman's series of books called, "The Language of God". (This 4-book set is only available at the Pillar of Enoch Ministry web site).

Enoch could read and understand the Mazzaroth.

1 Enoch 81:1-2
"And he said unto me: 'Observe, Enoch, these heavenly tablets, and read what is written hereon, and mark every individual fact.' And I observed the heavenly tablets, and read everything which was written (thereon) and understood everything, and read the book of all the deeds of mankind, and of all the children of flesh."

1 Enoch 93:1-2
"Yea, I Enoch will declare (them) unto you, my sons: According to that which appeared to me in the heavenly vision, and which I have known through the word of the holy angels, and have learnt from the heavenly tablets."

1 Enoch 103:1
*"I know a mystery and <u>have read the heavenly</u>
<u>tablets, and have seen the holy books</u>..."*

1 Enoch 106:18 -107:1
*"And after that there shall be still more
unrighteousness than that which was first
consummated on the Earth; for I know the
mysteries of the holy ones; **for He, the Lord,
has showed me and informed me**, and I
have read (them) in the heavenly tablets." "And
I saw written on them that generation upon
generation shall transgress, till a generation of
righteousness arises, and transgression is
destroyed and sin passes away from the
Earth..."*

"For He, the Lord has showed me and informed me..." The
Lord is a good teacher and it seems Enoch was a good
student. It's possible that those 300 years of 'walks' was
"on-the-job-training". Let's not wait to be 'taught of God'
(John 6:45).

John 6:45
[19] *In that day there will be an altar to the
Lord in the midst of the land of Egypt, and
a pillar to the Lord at its border.*

What will you learn when you start walking with God?

Enoch learned the messages in the stars and how to
preserve those mysteries. According to some traditions,
these two friends collaborated on the Great Pyramid – YHVH
as architect and Enoch as builder of the *Great Pyramid of
Giza, Egypt.

Isaiah 19: 19-20

[19] In that day there will be an altar to the Lord in the midst of the land of Egypt, and a pillar to the Lord at its border.

[20] And it will be a sign and a witness to the Lord of hosts in the land of Egypt; for they will cry to the Lord because of oppressors, and He will send them a savior, even a mighty one, and he will deliver them.

Jeremiah 32: 20

"God has set signs and wonders in the land of Egypt, even unto this day, and in Israel, and among other men; and has made Himself a Name, as at this day."

God has set signs in the heavens; God has set signs and wonders in the land of Egypt. Only He could design a marvel like the Great Pyramid. Two amazing, architectural-unrepeatable monuments stand in the midst of the land of Egypt on the Giza plateau, the Great Pyramid and the Sphinx.

God sets signs; God communicates.

He made the stars signs to display His messages; another means to communicate. He allows us to understand the stars. With this understanding, YHVH's friend built a pillar in Egypt as a sign on the earth, just like YHVH placed the stars in the firmament as signs above.

Another theory according to the first century works of the historian Josephus, the pyramids were built by the relatives of Enoch, the sons of Seth. They learned the language of the stars from Enoch or directly from Enoch's best Friend and built the pyramid to preserve the spiritual and scientific knowledge that they received. Other than being a geographical and architectural marvels, it has been noted that, the mathematical constant (pi), the shape of the earth, the earth's dimensions, star alignments, and other ancient knowledge has been preserved within the Great Pyramid of Giza. Water damage has been observed on the Great Pyramid. Could the pyramid been created to preserve righteous knowledge from being destroyed by the flood?

A second look leads to lasting fruit

In the summer of 1992, I lived in Israel. During my Middle East adventures, I visited Cairo and the Sinai. It is one thing to read about the pyramids; it is quite a different thing to run around in the desert and climb down into one. It was an amazing experience. The great pyramid is just outside the city of Cairo. I was unaware of all the marvels of the Giza plateau but standing in the heat in front of them, you are just in awe by their majesty. My mind filled with thoughts of all the movies and National Geographic documentaries. All those shows depicted thousands of slaves cutting stone blocks, pushing large stones up man-made ramps, and stacking them in perfect order. Most of those TV shows said that all pyramids, including the Great Pyramid of Giza, were burial chambers for Egyptian pharaohs. I believed that for many decades.

I now believe that the Great Pyramid's original intent was to be a sign of the greatness of YHVH. A monument, a sign in the desert pointing to our Creator. Now this is a new revelation to me but I came to it through my journey to understand the stars. You could say that my 'second look at the stars' revealed to me a different perspective of the origin and purpose of that pyramid in Cairo. I'm not sure of your thoughts about the topic but, when you go visit, you will say, "It truly is one of the Seven Wonders of the World".

After my personal tour of the Great Pyramid and the Sphinx, I went back to Israel via a short stay in the Sinai. I stayed in a little tent community on the Red Sea. I visited a monastery at the base of Mount Sinai and then climbed to the top of Mount Sinai. It wasn't actually a climb since someone had actually chiseled steps up most of the mountain. I wasn't able to stay on the mountain as long as Moses but I did spend a single night near the top of the mount. It was a clear night with a full moon and a sky full of stars, it is possible that this book was birthed that night.

Job 38: 4-6
4 Where were you when I laid the foundation of the earth? Declare to Me, if you have and know understanding.

5 Who determined the measures of the earth, if you know? Or who stretched the measuring line upon it?

*6 Upon what were the foundations of it fastened, or who laid its **cornerstone**,"*

According to an equal projection map, the Giza Pyramid is at the midpoint of the land of Egypt. Which also happens to be the geographical center of the world's land masses (aka the exact center of planet); thus, 'cornerstone' the previous reference in the thirty-eighth chapter of Job.

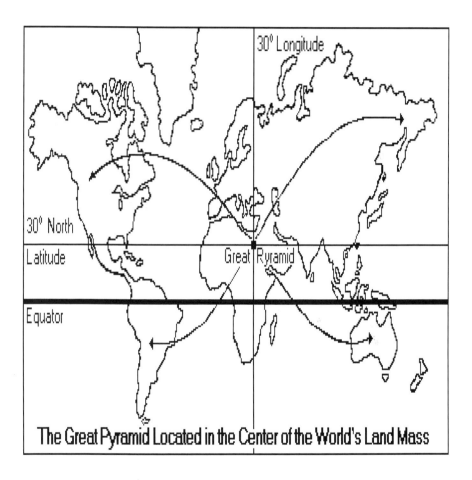

The Great Pyramid Located in the Center of the World's Land Mass

*(Note: For more details on the pyramid also see Joseph A. Seiss, "A Miracle in Stone" (1877))

Chapter 3 – The Magi

> Jeremiah 39:3 (AMP)
> ³ [When Jerusalem was taken] all the princes of the king of Babylon came in and sat in the Middle Gate: Nergal-sharezer, Samgar-nebo, Sarsechim [the Rabsaris] a chief of the eunuchs, and Nergal-sharezer [II, the Rabmag] a chief of the <u>magicians</u>, with all the rest of the officials of the king of Babylon.

> **Jeremiah 39:13 (AMP)**
> ¹³ So Nebuzaradan the captain of the guard, Nebushasban [the Rabsaris] a chief of the eunuchs, Nergal-sharezer [II, the Rabmag] a chief of the <u>magicians</u>, and all the chief officers of the king of Babylon

The two Old Testament words translated, "**magi**cian" are based upon the root word, "magi". The Magi were interpreters of omens and dreams; a practitioners of divination, magic, that included astrology, alchemy, and other forms of secret knowledge. History states, they were a class of priests among the Chaldeans, Persians, and Medes kings' council. They make their first biblical appearance in the book of Jeremiah as a King Nebuchadnezzar conquest.

A part of subduing a kingdom was to gather the magi (wise men) and religious teachers of the conquered foe. The Magi took their places among Nebuchadnezzar's "the astrologers and star gazers." It is with such men that, we understand that Daniel and his fellow exiles were "teamed with". Based on Daniel's exploits, he probably acquired the title, chief of the Magi, 'Rabmag' (Daniel 5:11).

18

Daniel 5:11 (AMP)

[11] There is a man in your kingdom in whom is the Spirit of the holy God [or gods], and in the days of your father light and understanding and wisdom like the wisdom of the gods were found in him; and King Nebuchadnezzar, your father— the king, I say, your father—appointed him master of the magicians, enchanters or soothsayers, Chaldeans, and astrologers,

Daniel's prophecies were legendary in and out of the kingdom. He actually looked to the heavens and provided calculations which he pointed to the very time when the Messiah would be born. His prophecies are in the book of Daniel and are also a part of other ancient literature.

Magi Roman History

The Roman historians Tacitus and Suetonius record, "…the advent of a great king who was to rise from among the Jews. It had fermented in the minds of men, heathen as well as Jews, and would have led them to welcome Jesus as the Christ had he come in accordance with their expectation."

Virgil, who lived a little before this, stated, "…a child from heaven was looked for, who should restore the golden age and take away sin. This expectation arose largely from the dispersion of the Jews among all nations, carrying with them the hope and the promise of a divine Redeemer." According to some other traditions, the Magi were represented by three kings, named Gaspar, Melchior and Belthazar."

The Original Star Search

In the New Testament, the Magi appear as "wise men" (also known as, Magians) who were guided by a star from "the east" to Jerusalem. Their journey led them to appear before Herod the Great. Following a star led them to seek the new-born king of the Jews, whom they had come to worship.

> **<u>Matthew 2: 1 - 12</u>**
> *¹Now when Jesus was born in Bethlehem of Judea in the days of Herod the king, behold, wise men [astrologers] from the east came to Jerusalem, asking,*
>
> *² Where is He Who has been born King of the Jews? <u>For we have seen His</u> **<u>star</u>** <u>in the east at its rising</u> and have come to worship Him.*
>
> *³ When Herod the king heard this, he was disturbed and troubled, and the whole of Jerusalem with him.*
>
> *⁴ So he called together all the chief priests and learned men (scribes) of the people and anxiously asked them where the Christ was to be born.*
>
> *⁵ They replied to him, In Bethlehem of Judea, for so it is written by the prophet:*
>
> *⁶ And you Bethlehem, in the land of Judah, you are not in any way least or insignificant among the chief cities of Judah; for from you shall come a Ruler (Leader) Who will govern and shepherd My people Israel.*

⁷ Then Herod sent for the wise men [astrologers] secretly, and accurately to the last point ascertained from them the time of the appearing of the star [that is, how long the star had made itself visible since its rising in the east].

⁸ Then he sent them to Bethlehem, saying, go and search for the Child carefully and diligently, and when you have found Him, bring me word, that I too may come and worship Him.

⁹ When they had listened to the king, they went their way, and behold, the star which had been seen in the east in its rising went before them until it came and stood over the place where the young Child was.

¹⁰ When they saw the star, they were thrilled with ecstatic joy.

¹¹ And on going into the house, they saw the Child with Mary His mother, and they fell down and worshipped Him. Then opening their treasure bags, they presented to Him gifts—gold and frankincense and myrrh.

¹² And receiving an answer to their asking, they were divinely instructed and warned in a dream not to go back to Herod; so they departed to their own country by a different way.

When you perceive the star or when you see what the stars are trying to tell you – you to will be **"thrilled with ecstatic joy"**. These men who gave the stars a second look were wise and rewarded. Following the star led these men to their high destiny.

The New Star Search

This portion of my journey started before I knew. I think all my stories start before I know what Abba is up to – it is good that He does not need my permission before a journey. I must have signed a 'non-expiring' permission slip early in my earth life or possibly before my earth existence.

Anyway, I must confess I have had many 'phobias' along the way. (Yes, that is tough to admit.) I think they are all based around some lack of understanding aka "a fear of the unknown". One day I think in 2012 or 2011, we were having another conversation about New Agers. It went something like:

> **Abba***: "Back in the time of Jesus' birth would you have been a friend of a Magi"*
>
> **Me:** *"Nope!"*
>
> **Abba***: "They were the first to really whole - heartedly seek and find me"*
>
> **Me:** *"Ummm, nope. Those guys were the original New Agers".*
>
> **Abba***: "Even, if they would have told you who/what they were seeking?"*
>
> **Me:** I recalled from some previous study, that these guys had journeyed for years (possibly two years or more). *With a little less pride, I*

22

said, "I can't imagine following a star". My mind was then flooded with years of Christmas plays, movies, and bedtime stories.

Then I recalled, the fact that I had actually volunteered to dress up as a Magi and walk the sidewalks of Washington DC to bring gifts to a baby in a manager. I participated in a living nativity scene. (If you do a diligent google search you will find pictorial evidence supporting my Christmas extra-curricular activities.)

Abba*:* The Lord seemed to watch me as replayed all the contents from my "Magi Files".

Abba*:* He repeated His original question, *"Would you have been a friend of a Magi?"*

Me: This time I did not answer because I realized He was actually serious about the question. Now, I pondered, *"Am I going back in time or am I going to meet a contemporary New Ager?*

This is a new age & New Agers are valuable!

The New Magi

Magi are people who have been trained in the art and science of understanding planetary alignments. The new magi are have an anointing to see the heavens from the Father's original intent, according to the names which the Father originally named each star. Since the "heavens declare the glory", all the names communicate significant meanings that can reveal and support your prophetic destiny.

YHVH has been looking with great expectation to see you respond to messages in the stars. Messages of identity, salvation, purpose, worth, overcoming victory, the gospel, destiny, and love. It is time for us to take a second look at the stars and to discover and live the message!

As the heavens declare the glory of God, I believe Liberating Ministries for Christ (LMCI) has the mandate to train and release **new magi** into the earth. I've received training, tasted the fruit of LMCI, and am now more equipped to run my race and to take my place. I know I am a "new mystic"; I am now acquainted with new magi(s).

If you desire additional insights and or training to equip you for your journey – please engage with the life and ministry, **Liberating Ministries for Christ International** (LMCI) of Dr. Dale Sides. His main website is www.lmci.org.

---

www.thenewmagi.com

24

Chapter 4 – Oh My Stars

Technology is so advanced now; that, it enables the contemporary magi to "follow the star" from the comfort of your home. One such space program for your stargazing is called, **Stellarium**. Stellarium [http://stellarium.org/] is a free open source "planetarium" accessible on your computer. This tool is your personal Hubble telescope, putting the stars at arm's reach. This tool can increase your astronomy skills and provide the Mazzaroth close-up. You can enter any month, day, year and journey through time to see the stars. If you enter September 11, 3 BC, you will see the constellations that were overhead during the time of Jesus' birth.

> "**Astronomy** is not only pleasant but also very useful to be known; it cannot be denied that this art unfolds the admirable wisdom of God." – John Calvin (1554)

Astronomy and **NOT** astrology!

John Calvin is a wise man. Simply stated astronomy is a tool of our Creator; while, astrology is a perversion of the original message. Un-corrected astrology is a study of twisted messages. Astrologers are evangelists of twisted star messages. Perversion is a **device** of the deceiver.

The Creator placed each star in the heavens with a reason and a purpose. One of those reasons was to communicate His Master plan to all mankind. The original intent of the star's placement was to be guide. They were placed in the sky to help people to return to and/or maintain their relationship with their Creator.

> **Genesis 1:14 (AMP)**
> *"And God said, Let there be lights in the expanse of the heavens to separate the day from the night, and **let them be signs and tokens [of God's provident care],** and [to mark] seasons, days, and years."*

Astronomy

> *"Astronomy? Impossible to understand and madness to investigate."*
> – Sophocles, c. 420 BC

> *"For everyone, as I think, must see that astronomy compels the soul to look upwards and leads us from this world to another."*
> – Glaucon, c. 380 BC

Astronomy is one of the oldest sciences and like most sciences it has both a foundation and is a foundation. A foundation that proves and supports the actions and desires of the Creator God. The earliest eastern civilizations such as the Babylonians, Greeks, Chinese, Indians, Iranians, and Mayans performed amazing observations and activities based on of the night sky. I think the Greek philosopher, Plato, had the right perspective. He said, "That anyone who studies (the night sky) must be convinced of the Divine Mind and or the Creator of the heavens."

*"Jewish tradition, preserved by the historian, Josephus, assures us that **biblical astronomy** was invented by Adam, Seth, and Enoch."*
- E.W. Bullinger (2009)

Over time, this glorious investigation of the beauty and mysteries captured in the stars became influenced by other forces, dark forces. Various cultures and groups replaced the innocent study of the stars with a new form of idolatry. People began to worship the stars as gods and began to look to the constellations for guidance. This became the breeding ground for different forms of divination, the birth of horoscopes, and the beginning of astrology.

There are other people who have chosen to believe that "the stars are signs". Signs used by the Creator to communicate messages to all mankind. Based upon the premise that the Creator communicates, some scientists have breathed a life back into astronomy and astrology. The subject, Christological Astronomy, is a book in itself. Dale Sides would be the subject matter expert on that topic. His website, www.christologicalastronomy.com, discusses the concept that our Creator has inscribed our individual destinies in the stars, just as the Creator has inscribed the complete gospel with the stars. I've attached my personal Level 1 Christological profile report (see the Appendix) as an example of the value of understanding the signs in the night sky.

A wealth of life at: www.christologicalastronomy.com

Astrology

Astrology is a perversion, a counterfeit of astronomy. Contemporary astrology tries to keep man from His Creator and focused on self. Astrology distracts one from true LIFE. It manipulates the purpose and message of the signs. It was not always perverted but people after the flood chose to believe that the Creator had stopped creating. People felt they were on their own so they separated the message from the Messenger. They began to interpret the signs without help or any assistance from the Creator. Independent readings became popular. Divining the future without the Divine became the norm. People turned from the Creator and turned to creation. The sun, moon, and the stars became the objects of worship. Horoscope reading is directly related to sun worship. The movement and the positions of these idols became important. The information was documented. It was used to provide guidance to those seeking "heavenly help". It has been reported, **"Astrological tables that are currently used were created over 2,300 years ago"**. Not only are they out of date but it seems that the position of the stars are also out of phase. The original creators of those tables were not able to account for the earth's movements through space. According to NASA, the planet earth has three basic movements relative to its celestial orientation: daily spinning; yearly revolutions, and persistent wobbling. The planet wobbles backwards on its axis every 26,000 years. The heavens and earth are not static. Everything is in motion; your life should not be static. Plus, recent technology shows that the earth's orientation to the stars changes one degree every 72 years. So most of the people who have tattooed their birth sign; have the wrong sign. The charts that astrologists use today to interpret the signs in the sky are inaccurate.

Horoscopes are derived from invalid Astrological tables

It is never good to try to be smarter than God or to assume what the Creator is trying to say. The technology was not available when the first "star mappers" created the first zodiac tables. The tables were based on what was visible to the eye not knowledge that was available from the Creator. Many in the current "astrology camp" have taken upon themselves to read the signs and produce a message that is **NOT** in alignment with the Creator's prime directive.

So the bad news is, "the current zodiac charts are old and wrong". The good news is the Creator's message for you is older than earth and more valuable than your body weight in gold.

Deuteronomy 4:19

19 And beware lest you lift up your eyes to the heavens, and when you see the sun, moon, and stars, even all the host of the heavens, you be drawn away and worship them and serve them, things which the Lord your God has allotted to all nations under the whole heaven.

Deuteronomy 18:10-14(KJV)

10 There shall not be found among you any one that maketh his son or his daughter to pass through the fire, or that useth divination, or an observer of times, or an enchanter, or a witch.

11 Or a charmer, or a consulter with familiar spirits, or a wizard, or a necromancer.

12 For all that do these things are an abomination unto the LORD: and because of these abominations the LORD thy God doth drive them out from before thee.

13 Thou shalt be perfect with the LORD thy God.

14 For these nations, which thou shalt possess, hearkened unto observers of times, and unto diviners: but as for thee, the LORD thy God hath not suffered thee so to do.

2 Kings 23:5 (AMP)
*5 He put away the idolatrous priests whom the kings of Judah had ordained to burn incense in the high places in Judah's cities and round about Jerusalem—also those who burned incense to Baal, **to the sun, to the moon, to the constellations [or twelve signs of the zodiac], and to all the hosts of the heavens**.*

So let's not confuse astronomy with astrology

Wikipedia says, "Astrology consists of several systems of divination based on the premise that there is a relationship between astronomical phenomena and events in the human world. In the West, astrology most often consists of a system of horoscopes purporting to explain aspects of a person's personality and predict future events in their life based on the positions of the sun, moon, and other celestial objects at the time of their birth. The majority of professional astrologers rely on such systems. Astrology has been dated to at least the 2nd millennium BCE."

Again, astronomy is a tool of our Creator; while, astrology is a perversion of astronomy.

Astrology has become an evil **DEVICE** to deceive, confuse, and attempts to seduce mankind into bondage and servitude.

Devices

The definitions of the word, 'wiles': *a trick, artifice, or stratagem meant to fool, trap, or entice; a* **device**. History has shown us how the enemy is consistently trying to fool, trap, and entice humans. The enemy will use any **device** to gain an advantage over man. It seems it is the enemy's goal to: get us dependent upon ourselves only, or to cause a division in our relationship with the YHVH or cause us to doubt His words. Only through revelation from a relationship with the Father, can we have any advantage over the enemy.

Our true victories ONLY come from union with Father.

> ### Isaiah 32:7 (AMP)
> *The instruments and methods of the fraudulent and greedy [for gain] are evil; he devises wicked* ***devices*** *to ruin the poor and the lowly with lying words, even when the plea of the needy is just and right.*

> ### 2 Corinthians 2:11 (AMP)
> *To keep Satan from getting the advantage over us; for we are not ignorant of his* ***wiles*** *and intentions.*

Like a scientist, the subtle, crafty enemy also finds a subject, introduces slight adjustments, observes the results, and makes more adjustments. The subtle serpent introduced questions into Eve's mind and over time Eve adjusted to the

31

serpent's programming. The enemy's object was to move Eve from a lover of God to a doubter of God. I do not believe this transaction occurred in one encounter. The enemy identified its subject and began its programming by introducing subtle adjustments. Most scientist document their activity; I believe we can read the details of enemy's setup and execution of the here:

Genesis 3:1-6 (AMP)

3 Now the serpent was more subtle *and* crafty than any living creature of the field which the Lord God had made. And he [Satan] said to the woman, Can it really be that God has said, You shall not eat from every tree of the garden?
2 And the woman said to the serpent, We may eat the fruit from the trees of the garden,
3 Except the fruit from the tree which is in the middle of the garden. God has said, You shall not eat of it, neither shall you touch it, lest you die.
4 But the serpent said to the woman, You shall not surely die,
5 For God knows that in the day you eat of it your eyes will be opened, and you will be like God, knowing the difference between good and evil *and* blessing and calamity.
6 And when the woman saw that the tree was good (suitable, pleasant) for food and that it was delightful to look at, and a tree to be desired in order to make one wise, she took of its fruit and ate; and she gave some also to her husband, and he ate.

This type of programming not only re-positioned Eve but it also led to Adam renouncing his seat of dominion. When the seat became vacant, the enemy sought to lord over that area of influence. Over time, the enemy has compiled strategies that utilize frequency, emotions, sin, circumstances, and other means to influence men and women.

The enemy fills his "tool bag" with **devices** that have been proven.

The enemy seeks to use his **devices** on independent individuals.

As stated earlier: the sun, moon, and the stars were given with the original intent to rule over the day and night

Genesis 1:16 (AMP)

[16] And God made the two great lights—
the greater light (the sun) **to rule** the day
and the lesser light (the moon) **to rule** the
night. He also made the stars.

I believe the enemy has also subtly been using people to re-program the "sun, moon and the stars". The enemy has used people to alter the messages or the meanings of the messages in the stars. Or maybe slight distortions to the names of the star, thus altering the messages. For example, the grouping of stars called Orion in ancient days was a sign of the delivering biblical Messiah. In current days, astrologers and diviners say that the Orion constellation can be interpreted as a symbol of strength and independence from authority.

It may be another enemy strategy to use several techniques including astrology, as **devices** for mankind's detriment.

Orion

Recently during a walk to my car, I was looking up at the constellation Orion. As I connected the 'dots' and traced the stars to form the constellation, I heard in my mind:

> *"From now on, when you look up to Orion, it'll remind you of your life of victory!*
>
> *You also have the option to function at that size, the physical size of that constellation, when you are active in My Kingdom!"*

I pondered that wonderfully, disruptive thought. I was reminded about the ten spies in book of Numbers (Num 13:33) who said, "We see ourselves as grasshoppers in their eyes." From that encounter, I now look and see myself as a giant in my Father's eyes. This has had a profound impact on my life and how I engage in every encounter. Many revelations you have with the Father are about your identity. It is important to know how the Father sees us. And equally, important is for us to believe Him and see ourselves as He sees us. And maybe still even more important, that we act on those beliefs that are founded on things revealed to us by our Father.

Matthew 16:17 (AMP)
¹⁷ Then Jesus answered him, Blessed are you, Simon Bar-Jonah. For flesh and blood [men] <u>have not revealed this to you, but My Father Who is in heaven</u>.

The Father original revealed Orion to me in an angelic encounter, for more detail see my third book, "*A Mystical Introduction To Angels*". In the course of my 'magi training' learning about constellations, I found that several planets in my "birth-sky" are also aligned near the Orion constellation.

Chapter 5 – Birth-sky

The Stellarium program allows you to see the birth-sky of our Messiah. The birth-sky declares the glory of heaven. Jesus' birth-sky is the gospel written with stars and planets. As the Father wrote Jesus' story, He has also written your story. As you can read Jesus' birth-sky, you can also read your own birth-sky (see the Appendix).

A birth-sky is comprised of the three components:
  I.   Your birth date and hour
  II. The 13 constellations (Mazzaroth). We are alive during a time of great revelation; even the revealing of another constellation. Current technology observes thirteen constellations not the traditional twelve:

Traditional Astrology Dates			Correct Astronomy Dates		
Zodiac	Dates	Days	Constellation	Dates	Days
Aries	21 Mar - 19 Apr	30	Aries	19 Apr – 13 May	25
Taurus	20 Apr - 20 May	31	Taurus	14 May - 19 Jun	37
Gemini	21 May - 20 Jun	31	Gemini	20 Jun - 20 Jul	31
Cancer	21 Jun - 22 Jul	32	Cancer	21 Jul – 9 Aug	20
Leo	23 Jul - 22 Aug	31	Leo	10 Aug – 15 Sep	37
Virgo	23 Aug - 22 Sep	31	Virgo	16 Sep – 30 Oct	45
Libra	23 Sep - 22 Oct	30	Libra	31 Oct – Nov 22	23
Scorpio	23 Oct - 21 Nov	30	Scorpius	23 Nov - 29 Nov	7
			Ophiuchus	30 Nov - 17 Dec	18
Sagittarius	22 Nov - 21 Dec	30	Sagittarius	18 Dec - 18 Jan	32
Capricorn	22 Dec - 19 Jan	29	Capricornus	19 Jan - 15 Feb	28
Aquarius	20 Jan - 18 Feb	30	Aquarius	16 Feb – 11 Mar	24
Pisces	19 Feb - 20 Mar	30-31	Pisces	12 Mar - 18 Apr	38

These dates are from: http://dionysia.org/astrology/sun-signs.html

III.   The Sun, Moon, and the 9 "real" planets. We are living in an era of amazing knowledge and revelation. I'm still wrestling with the fact that Pluto is no longer regarded as a 'real' planet. Pluto was first discovered and classified as planet in 1930. Pluto lost its "real planet status" by the International Astronomical Union in 2006. There is a rumor in the scientific community that there is movement to reinstate Pluto. Current astrology and my magi friends recognize these ten planets:

1. Mercury
2. Venus
3. Earth
4. Mars
5. Ceres
6. Jupiter
7. Saturn
8. Neptune
9. Uranus

Ceres is not traditionally listed with the "real planets". Ceres is added to the list because it supports Saturn's name of the "7th planet" and it maybe the remains of a previously destroyed planet. If you have access the Stellarium program, you can see the birth-sky of Jesus if you enter September 11, 2 BC instead of 3 BC, this adjustment is just for his birthday not yours.

Your birth-sky tells of His design of your destiny

Chapter 6 – Astrology and Encumbrances

> **Hebrews 12:1 (AMP)**
> *"Therefore then, since we are surrounded by so great a cloud of witnesses [who have borne testimony to the Truth], let us strip off and throw aside every **encumbrance** (unnecessary weight) and that sin which so readily (deftly and cleverly) clings to and entangles us, and let us run with patient endurance and steady and active persistence the appointed course of the **race** that is set before us."*

According to the above verse, "every encumbrance and sin" are things that hinder our ability to run our **race**.

Race = successfully living unto the Lord Most High

We all have clear understandings of sin but little understanding of **encumbrances**.   I believe as we take responsibility for our destinies and look to the stars, we will gain understanding and be able to deal with "every **encumbrance**".

I am finding there are many **encumbrances** in life; well maybe just my life. I believe every one born from human parents receives **encumbrances**, unnecessary weights. This occurs twice: once at your conception and a second time at your birth.

If you are running your race without any weights – please skip this chapter and contact me for a full refund.

Gate Keeping

Galatians 4:1
*Now what I mean is that as long as the inheritor is a child and under age, he does not differ from a **slave**, although he is the master of all the estate;*

Again, I believe we, mere humans, pick up "extra weight" when <u>we **enter** and **exit** the womb</u>. Not only were we a slave to sin but we are also <u>subject to time</u> and <u>suppressed by the ruling stars</u>.

We are more than just the joining of a sperm and an egg. At the moment that the sperm and egg join, your spirit being also joins them. Before that moment, you were outside of time; after that moment, chronos (time) became your weight.

Time is a weight

Genesis 1:16-18 (AMP)
*[16] And God made the two great lights— the greater light (**the sun**) to rule the day and the lesser light (**the moon**) to rule the night. He also made **the stars**.*

[17] And God set them in the expanse of the heavens to give light upon the earth,

*[18] **To rule over the day and over the night**, and to separate the light from the darkness. And God saw that it was good (fitting, pleasant) and He approved it.*

Astronomy, or better said, Christological Astronomy proposes that the Creator's placement of the sun and the position of the moon (your birth-sky) are significant. Their location on your day of your birth produces a divine message. This personal message (properly read and understood) will provide prophetic insights into your divine destiny in the field of stars.

Approximately nine months after conception, you exit inner space. In phase II, you come into outer space which is under the stars, specifically a grouping of stars in which the sun & moon are uniquely positioned. You are under submission to the Mazzaroth at birth. This enslavement is regardless whether a person plays with their daily horoscope or astrology or any other form of divination. So, at birth your zodiac sign became the symbol of 'lord of your house'. The stars have influence and some 'rule' over you.

Programmed stars are cruel masters

Isaiah 28:6 (AMP)
[6] And a spirit of justice to him who sits in judgment *and* administers the law, and **strength to those who turn back the battle at the gate**.

Places of Battle	Enemy
Time Gate	Coming out of **eternity** and into earth makes TIME your master
Womb Gate	Coming out of **security** and into the world system makes FEAR your master

Redeeming the time

Ephesians 5:15-17 (New Century Version)
[15] So be very careful how you live. Do not live like those who are not wise, but live wisely.

[16] Use every chance you have for doing good, because these are evil times.

*[17] So do not be foolish **but learn** what the Lord wants you to do.*

I'm in agreement with being careful how to live and living wisely, but how does one 'live wisely' in the light of our human condition? According to the word above, we have the capacity and the permission to do 'good' in these 'evil times'. Through this, we can actually redeem the times in our lives.

In this context, "**redeem**" means:

1. To compensate for the faults or bad aspects of something.
2. To gain or regain possession of something in exchange for payment.

On the topic of redeeming time, I've had some interesting conversations. A few years ago during a conversation, some friends told me they had spent time and energy repenting for each day of their life. I marveled, but thought that was too much effort. Later that year, another friend notified me that he was going to "redeem the time" and repent for each month of his life. I thought that was a lot of months and a good activity for him but again not for me.

One of the purposes of this book is to share what I have learned and learning from the Lord on regaining possession of time. Maybe better said, "Let's understand our correct relationship with time and the zodiac". The enemy has been using time as its ally. The enemy is not creative but strategic and very manipulative. The enemy looks for **devices** to use against mankind. The enemy can use time against us. So "manipulated time" could be a device of the enemy.

> ### Job 38:31-33 (AMP)
> *31 Can you bind the chains of [the cluster of stars called] Pleiades, or loose the cords of [the constellation] Orion?*
>
> *32 Can you lead forth the signs of the zodiac (Mazzaroth) in their season? Or can you guide [the stars of] the Bear with her young?*
>
> *33 Do you know the ordinances of the heavens? Can you **establish their rule** upon the earth?*

We learned from Enoch's interactions that there are benefits to having a relationship with God. As you spend time with the Father, you learn a lot. It is one thing when you ask the Lord a question. It is something completely different when He asks you a question. You learn that His questions are the best learning aides. His questions are "leading" questions. If you engage properly, they can lead to some amazing places.

Questions from the Lord are tools to remind you of your true identity. His motive is to correct your thinking. As a man thinks in his heart so is he. Your motive for questions is usually knowledge. His motive is transition and transformation. One day I was pondering a concept: "being over time and not under time..." Then He interrupted my thoughts with a question, **"So you want to be a time lord?"** I responded by repeating the question. I'm thinking that this maybe a key to walking with God as Enoch did. (Hmmm, have I unlocked the mystery of relationship with the Creator?) Anyway, I repeated the question He asked me, "**You want to be a time lord?**" When I did, I began to believe. I began to believe it was possible to actually redeem time. The questions opened the door to faith and the belief, "**I can be Over Time**" walk in that open door. Yes, I had faith to believe I could master time and make time subservient.

Time is my servant; time will work for me.

"Write the vision, so you can run with it..." A plan formed. I wrote it. I did it. I got my journal out and made a list of all the days that my birth was celebrated. Starting with **May 17, 1962**. Here is a rewrite of my plan to redeem time. Following this plan, I received the "gift of time" on my 2014 birthday.

Step 1: Birthday Table

Birthday Table			
May 1963	May 1976	May 1989	May 2002
May 1964	May 1977	May 1990	May 2003
May 1965	May 1978	May 1991	May 2004
May 1966	May 1979	May 1992	May 2005
May 1967	May 1980	May 1993	May 2006
May 1968	May 1981	May 1994	May 2007
May 1969	May 1982	May 1995	May 2008
May 1970	May 1983	May 1996	May 2009
May 1971	May 1984	May 1997	May 2010
May 1972	May 1985	May 1998	May 2011
May 1973	May 1986	May 1999	May 2012
May 1974	May 1987	May 2000	May 2013
May 1975	May 1988	May 2001	May 2014

Step 2: Declarations:

I spent 10 minutes redeeming each of my birthday months, which represented each year of my life:

- *"I Take This Time!"*

- *"I am NOW on this day of [17 May YYYY] born of God and He who is born of God overcomes the world"*

- *"This is the Day the Lord Has made – I rejoice & I am glad"*

- *"I present myself to my High Priest, Jesus, as a living sacrifice"*

- *"I acknowledge You as the Author & Finisher of my faith!"*

- *"Solomon was wrong – there is something NEW under the sun!"*

- *"I am altogether new! Because, I am HIS WORKMANSHIP created, recreated in Christ Jesus"*

- *"I am no longer under chronos!"*

- *"I am no longer in chaos!"*

- *As You open my scroll – I am empowered to walk in Kairos"*

- *"I TAKE this Day captive!"*

- *"I TAKE this MONTH captive!"*

- *"I TAKE this YEAR captive"*

- *"And I place this record of my birth in submission to my scroll of Destiny as the High Council intended for me to be…"*

I had written out those statements as I started repossessing the 1st month and added a few statements along the way. It was tough reclaiming this territory, but it was well worth the effort. I walked in this process to be the unique son of God that I was called to be.

> With each birth-day that I reclaimed – **I was becoming whole, the son of God** that I was designed to be.

Step 3: Journaling:
You should be ready to record the results of your activity. Journaling is a good habit to get into. I started noticing a difference in me somewhere around addressing the half-way point (May 1986). I could see myself with the "Household" of the Kingdom; it felt like I was actually re-aligning. Here are some excerpts from my journaling, recorded the results during and after the declarations:

- *When I reached <u>May 1990</u>, I was reminded of the Jet Li movie, "The One" (2001). In this movie, the anti-hero spends his time entering alternative universes and kills his alternate personas. The anti-hero grows stronger, faster, and smarter each time he eliminated a version of himself. I'm not glorying in the killing but reflecting on the beauty of not being fragmented.*

- *When I reclaimed May <u>1992</u>, I had the ability to look down on my timeline and I could see the beginning and the end.*

- *When I reclaimed May <u>2001</u>, I saw myself walking on a path. I was walking with 'fire-*

beings'. Before we walked very far, the beings gave me garments of fire so that I could wear them in order to continue my journey.

- *When I reclaimed May 2009, I recall hearing, "His blood still speaks; His blood in you is always saying, "draw near, and come close to me!"*

- *When I reclaimed May 2014, I perceived that I would have more involvement with the 7 Spirits of God this year and later on my birthday I saw them standing in a circle around me; hands clasped. They danced and rejoiced over me.*

Hebrews 2:8 (AMP)
*8 For You (GOD) have put everything in subjection under his feet. Now in putting everything in subjection to man, **He (GOD) left nothing outside of man's control.** But at present we do not yet see all things subjected to him [man].*

GOD left nothing outside of man's control.

Many of us don't believe this. Many of us are hiding behind a false understanding of sovereignty. Despite our thoughts, this is still truth for all on the planet. The truth of sovereignty is that our Sovereign God has sovereignly delegated His authority to us. **Will you believe the Sovereign and take responsibility over your domain?**

Will you ACT on these truths?

IT WILL TAKE FAITH. I recommend becoming a "believing believer who believes" (see Steve Backlund's books, videos, and audios).

Every act of **faith is worth** the effort

This one definitely was. I'm not sure if I will tackle every month of my life or every day of my life. But I definitely know these were positive steps taken on my journey. We can all grow more mature by taking responsibility for time and our life.

I am experiencing a new level of freedom. I do recommend that you meditate on the Truth, make some declarations, and in some manner, **redeem the time**!

Ephesians 5:16 (KJV)
^{16} *redeeming the time, because the days are evil.*

Imperium Tempus (Control Time)

Facebook does have some redeeming qualities. On my May 2014 birthday after I finished my redeeming activity, I found this word posted:

"The Father says, today be lifted up! Be lifted up you EVERLASTING GATE for the KING OF GLORY is coming in – I am the king of the glory on the inside of you says the Father and it is My intent to put your foot on the neck of your enemy.

You have been lied to and you have been betrayed. You have been set at naught and overlooked. You have been criticized and you have been marginalized.

I am about to bring you to center stage in a powerful move of My spirit that will redefine for those around you what GLORY and POWER in the things of God. Open your mouth wide and I will fill it! I will make you my battle axe and my weapon of war. I will send you into the fray and into the battle and you will come back with the spoil and bring captivity captive.

You will dismantle illegitimate authority and release the captives says the Father for that is your mandate and your assignment and I will be so disposed as to back you up. Your whole life will be transformed by your obedience to the task that I set before you this day."

May 17th, 2014 by Russell Walden

Chapter 7 – Take Your Place

John 8:31-32 (AMP)

[31] So Jesus said to those Jews who had believed in Him, If you abide in My word **[hold fast to My teachings and live in accordance with them]**, you are truly My disciples.

[32] And you will know the Truth, and the Truth will set you **free**.

If you have done your part in redeeming the time, then you are abiding in His word. We have a part; He has a part in our freedom. Even though our part is very small, we still have a critical role in our liberty. By being a doer of the word and not just reading words, you are 'holding fast to His teachings and actually living in accordance with them'. This is one way that we do our part in being free.

If you have 'redeemed the time' and are free from the control of time, **you are free to take your PLACE.** In this PLACE, you learn to know (or remember) the ordinances of the heavens. With this revelation and under godly lordship, you can establish righteous rule upon the earth from your PLACE in the heavens.

Job 38:33 (AMP)
[33] *Do you know the ordinances of the heavens? Can you establish their rule upon the earth?*

> **Sign of the zodiac** (noun) – in astrology one of 13 equal areas into which the zodiac is divided;
> **Synonyms:** mansion, **planetary <u>house</u>**, star sign, sign, **house**

Some astrology systems divide the constellations into groupings called the zodiac. Mazzaroth is the Hebrew word for constellations or zodiac. Each zodiac sign has a corresponding **house**. I believe each house was created to be ruled and there are no empty seats of rule. I believe; each **house** has a steward or a ruler; some astrologers say that a designated planet rules the **house**. I believe; sons were predestined to rule these houses. I believe; we need to at least rule the house of our birth-sky.

Romans 8:15 (AMP)
15 For [the Spirit which] you have now received [is] not a spirit of slavery to put you once more **in bondage to fear**, but you have received the Spirit of adoption [the Spirit producing sonship] in [the bliss of] which we cry, Abba (Father)! Father!

If we are not occupying the seat, then the there is usually an illegal or incompetent ruler in our place. Our ignorance or lack of knowledge or the <u>bondage to fear</u> has led to us forsaking or not occupying our rightful places, the seat of rule. His Spirit is producing sonship; we are maturing sons. I declare, we are no longer ignorant and we are well able.

Who is the **rightful lord** of the HOUSE?

Lordship

Psalm 8:6 (AMP)
6 You (YHVH) made him to have dominion over the works of Your hands; You (YHVH) have put all things under his feet:

Our elder brother, the first Adam, had dominion over all created things. The last Adam had dominion over all created things. Time and the stars are creations of our Creator. It's a family tradition to have dominion over all created things. This is one good tradition that I expect to walk in! As we walk in the family tradition we will have loyal subjects

---
Loyal subjects are excellent servants of righteous lords

We are DESTINED to have dominion.

We are DESTINED to rule.

1 Timothy 6:15
*"Which [appearing] will be shown forth in His own proper time by the blessed, only Sovereign (Ruler), the King of kings and the **Lord of lords**,"*

Revelation 17:14
*"They will wage war against the Lamb, and the Lamb will triumph over them; for He is **Lord of lords** and King of kings— and those with Him and on His side are chosen and called [elected] and loyal and faithful followers."*

Revelation 19:16
*"And on His garment (robe) and on His thigh He has a name (title) inscribed, King of kings and **Lord of lord**s."*

Does **He** not **call us** lords?

Are the heavens a place where you sit as lord of the house? Can Jesus' title, Lord of lords, be fulfilled?

It seems that there may be others lording over the house. I've heard some folks say, "Angels are holding our thrones (places of ruler ship) until we mature and take our place. I hope that is the case and that they are patient. But I have yet to find written or audible confirmation that supports this hope. I have found the following charge:

> **Zechariah 3:7**
> *[7] Thus says the Lord of hosts: If you will walk in My ways and keep My charge, **then also you shall rule My house** and have charge of My courts, and I will give you access to My presence and places to walk among these who stand here.*

Until we walk in His ways and keep His charge, others (none kingdom family members) **will rule in our place.** We may be His paramount creation pre-planned to rule but we can NOT expect to be lords if we do not follow His ways. We are designed (created) in His image but we must be transfigured into His Likeness. Simply said, "**We must follow the Leader!**"

Romans 8:14 (AMP)

14 For all who are led by the Spirit of God are sons of God.

Many will be deceived and deluded and will think that the way to this place of lordship is by "working their way to the top". That method will only lead to fatigue, depression, and premature death. We are made lords by believing His words, walking in His ways, and growing in intimate relationship.

Master and Steward

There is a relationship between the "Master and the steward" that would benefit all those who are seeking to walk in the ways of the Kingdom. If we do not clearly understand this from a kingdom perspective, we will miss opportunities and not function or fit well in the kingdom:

Matthew 20: 1- 8

*1"For the Kingdom of Heaven is like a man who was the **master of a household**, who went out early in the morning to hire laborers for his vineyard.*

2 When he had agreed with the laborers for a denarius a day, he sent them into his vineyard.

3 He went out about the third hour, and saw others standing idle in the marketplace.

4 To them he said, 'You also go into the vineyard, and whatever is right I will give you.' So they went their way.

⁵ Again he went out about the sixth and the ninth hour, and did likewise.

⁶ About the eleventh hour he went out, and found others standing idle. He said to them, 'Why do you stand here all day idle?'

⁷ They said to him, 'Because no one has hired us.' He said to them, 'You also go into the vineyard, and you will receive whatever is right.'

*⁸ When evening had come, the lord of the vineyard said to his **steward**, 'Call the laborers and pay them their hire, beginning from the last to the first.'*

If you **respond to Him**, you receive!

Love

If you LOVE ME, you will keep my commandments. Or a good steward may say, "**Love is the method that will enable you to walk in His ways**."

LOVE will motivate you to keep His charge!

And as stated earlier, if you keep His charge, then also you will rule His House. You WILL have dominion over the works of His hands!

Daniel 11:32 (AMP)

*And such as violate the covenant he shall pervert and seduce with flatteries, **but the people who know their God** shall prove themselves strong and shall stand firm and do exploits [for God].*

Love is the only means!

Love is the secret to success in the Real Kingdom, but now the secret is out. We have no more excuses. We are all candidates to sit in the heavens and to rule.

LOVE is the ticket to **DOMINION.**

With intimate, active, engaging with your Heavenly Father, you will become like Him - a Mighty Ruling King.

**LOVE
never fails
to transform man
into his highest place!**

Star Dream

> ### Genesis 37:9 (AMP)
> *9But Joseph dreamed yet another dream and told it to his brothers [also]. He said, See here, I have dreamed again, and behold, [this time not only] eleven <u>stars</u> <u>[but also] the sun and the moon </u>bowed down and did reverence to me!*

Let's see how this star dream manifested. The life of Joseph is filled with many beneficial lessons. We are going to focus on his time in Egypt. This scene from Joseph's life will demonstrate how **a friend of God** lives in the midst of an evil day (see Ephesians 5:16) and anti-Christ culture. He will demonstrate how one should behave in "another's house". Life is NOT the same for a man that the Lord is with. Forcefully taken from his homeland, he landed in the house of an Egyptian named, Potiphar.

Interestingly, the Hebrew meaning of Potiphar is "he who Ra gave". In Egypt, Ra was worshipped as the "mighty" sun god. Ra was masquerading and seeking to be hallowed as creator. When the Almighty identifies a usurper, He sends a **Dread Champion** to confront, conqueror, and reign victorious. <u>Son of God is another name for **Dread Champion**</u>.

> ### John 3:16 (NKJV)
> *16 For God so loved the world that <u>He gave His only begotten Son</u>, that whoever believes in Him should not perish but have everlasting life.*

Jesus is "He who Abba gave". He was sent to earth to destroy the works of the devil (**1 John 3:8**). Jesus is a Dread Champion. We know His winning record. Our Creator placed Joseph in that house to confront the gods of Egypt. Joseph is "he who Abba gave. I believe we should do similar as we take our place in the celestial houses and every house He leads us to.

We are to rule in EVERY House

Genesis 39:2 - 5 (AMP)
*2But **the Lord was with Joseph,** and he [though a slave] was a successful and prosperous man; and he was in the **house** of his master the Egyptian.*

3And his master saw that the Lord was with him and that the Lord made all that he did to flourish and succeed in his hand.

*4So Joseph pleased [Potiphar] and found favor in his sight, and he served him. And [his master] made him supervisor over his **house** and he put all that he had in his charge.*

*5From the time that he made him **supervisor in his house and over all that he had,** the Lord blessed the Egyptian's house for Joseph's sake; and **the Lord's blessing was on all that he had in the house and in the field.***

Again, <u>until we walk in His ways</u> and keep His charge, others will rule in our place. Joseph's star dream said he would eventually be a man of influence. The Egyptians and their false gods were ruling the world, but Joseph believed the message in his star dream. **Joseph is a Dread Champion**. Joseph was sent to save the world and the world he did save. We have the privilege to rule in His stead.

The path to being a **Dread Champion** begins by being led.

Genesis 37:9 (AMP)
9But Joseph dreamed yet another dream and told it to his brothers [also]. He said, See here, I have dreamed again, and behold, [this time not only] eleven <u>stars</u> <u>[but also] the sun and the moon </u>bowed down and did reverence to me!

The star dream was a vision of government rule. Stars, the sun, and the moon in submission to a lord. His dream was a truth and a motivation that helped Joseph to become the most powerful person on the planet. He may lead through dreams or even the stars in the sky. Will you follow the Dread Champion wherever and however He leads? (Read the details of the journey in **Genesis 41**) I believe **Dread Champions** are made as they walk in His Ways and keep His charge.

Genesis 41:40 (NKJV)
*40 **You shall be over my house,** and all my people shall be ruled according to your word; only in regard to the throne will I be greater than you.*

Follow His lead, take your place; displace principalities, and become a **Dread Champion**

Displacement Theology

You can go to Wikipedia and find a definition for the word "displacement" and the word "theology" or you can accept my definition for "displacement theology". I define "displacement theology" as a stronger one 'dis-placing' an illegal squatter. It can also be an activity motivated by love that occurs when an entity enters a 'place' and pushes another entity out of the place it was occupying and thus taking its place.

> ### Exodus 20:3 (AMP)
> *³You shall have no other gods <u>before or besides</u> Me.*

Based upon my understanding of displacement theology, Yeshua came to remove any other gods before and besides YHVH. Some entity was sitting in the gate. Jesus displaced that entity so we could enter through that gate. Now, we can return to our first estate.

The foundation for this theology can be seen in the world's favorite bible verse, John 3:17 – "For God sent not his Son into the world to condemn the world; but that the world through Him might be saved." It seems the Father sent Yeshua into the world to displace another god, so that there would not be any gods before or beside Him.

> ### 1 John 3:8 (AMP)
> *"...the reason the Son of God was made manifest (visible) was to **undo** (destroy, loosen, and dissolve) the works the devil [has done]."*

Two things cannot exist in the same place

Yeshua came to undo the works of enemy. I believe "undo" aligns with displacement. The son of God became manifested so that he could displace the enemy and take back the place that Adam lost. The Father's actions; the Son's actions open the door for us to enter in and displace the adversary in our individual worlds.

Actions follow beliefs

The original ruling one, Adam, did not guard and keep his LOVE with the Father. Not in love, not in union – Adam forfeited his throne. He lost his ruling place in the house.

> ### Jude 1:21
> "Guard and keep yourselves in the love of God..."

Jesus **guarded** His self and **stayed** in love with God. Jesus kept Himself in the love of God. Staying in love requires action on our part. Jesus' union with the Father empowered Him to live & to displace the enemy. I believe this current generation of sons will manifest the same behavior of being strong in the Lord.

> ### Ephesians 6:10
> "In conclusion, be strong in the Lord **[be empowered through your union with Him]**; draw your strength from Him [that strength which His boundless might provides]."

As stated earlier in Zechariah 3, **if you keep His charge**, then also you will rule His House and have dominion over the works of His hands! **Enoch kept His charge. Joseph kept His charge. Jesus kept His charge.**

This generation **will keep** His charge.

We **will keep** His charge.

You **will keep** His charge.

I **will keep** His charge.

Zechariah 3:7
*[7] Thus says the Lord of hosts: If you will walk in My ways and keep My charge, **then also you shall rule My house** and have charge of My courts, and I will give you access to My presence and places to walk among these who stand here.*

If you **stay in Love with Him**, you will keep His charge

Chapter 8 – Attributes

<u>Genesis 22:17 </u>(AMP)
*"And such as violate the covenant he
shall pervert and seduce with flatteries,
<u>BUT the people who know</u> their God
shall prove themselves strong and shall
stand firm and do exploits [for God]."*

To be effective on this planet, many experts have tied future success with intelligence. **BUT,** I would say it's about who **you know**. Let me introduce a new concept called "spiritual intelligence". **Spiritual intelligence** is somewhat similar to emotional intelligence but it is the ability to understand one's own and other entity's knowledge of information not acquired through intellect or other natural senses but acquired through divine interaction. You will find this definition in Wikipedia. One has a 'high' spiritual intelligence quotient (IQ) if one uses this intelligence for living this life on earth and other realms.

What's your spiritual IQ?

I think spiritual IQ was addressed a few years ago by another mystical writer, Paul. He wrote, *"Now concerning* **spirituals***, I would not have you ignorant." (1 Corinthians 12:1)* For the most part, I don't think we have heeded Paul's concerns. Under the broad topic of **spirituals**, I believe we have been most ignorant on the subtopic of "the life and activities of spirit beings". Many have fortified their ignorance by reading the bible from a natural mindset and NOT reading it from an active knowledge of God. In our ignorance, we have had a tendency to believe that every spiritual creature identified in the bible is an angel.

Based upon some spiritual intelligence, I propose that, "stars" are not angels but stars are another class of spiritual being. Yes, I know that in the New Testament there are a couple inferences:

Revelation 1:20 (KJV)
*"The mystery of the seven **stars** which thou sawest in my right hand, and the seven golden candlesticks. **The seven stars are the angels** of the seven churches: and the seven candlesticks which thou sawest are the seven churches."*

Revelation 12:3-4 (KJV)
3 And there appeared another wonder in heaven; and behold a great red dragon, having seven heads and ten horns, and seven crowns upon his heads.

*4 And his tail drew **the third part of the stars of heaven**, and did cast them to the earth: and the dragon stood before the woman which was ready to be delivered, for to devour her child as soon as it was born.*

Because of those scriptures, we make the logical conclusion that stars are angels. But on a second look at **Revelations 1:20**, those seven stars are the cluster of seven stars in the Orion constellation. This cluster, known as the Pleiades, is also referenced in Amos:

Amos 5:8 (KJV)
"Seek him that maketh the seven stars and Orion, and turneth the shadow of death into the morning, and maketh the day dark with night: that calleth for the waters of the sea, and poureth them out upon the face of the earth: The Lord is his name:"

To increase your **Spiritual IQ**, do not base your understanding upon traditions; remove ignorance by being a workman who acquires information motivated by his divine union.

2 Timothy 2:15 (KJV)
*"Study and be eager and do your utmost to present yourself to God approved (tested by trial), a **workman** who has no cause to be ashamed, correctly analyzing and accurately dividing [rightly handling and skillfully teaching] the Word of Truth."*

Be a person who knows the Creator God

Ascending and Descending

Genesis 28:12 (AMP)
*"And he dreamed that there was a ladder set up on the earth, and the top of it reached to heaven; and the **angels of God** were **ascending** and **descending** on it!"*

John 1:51 (AMP)
*"Then He said to him, I assure you, most solemnly I tell you all, you shall see heaven opened, and the **angels of God ascending** and **descending** upon the Son of Man!"*

These Old and New Testament verses are intriguing. I've heard much teaching on the angelic. I even wrote a book on angels, *"A Mystical Introduction to Angels"*. A few months after finishing the book, I was encouraged to go a little deeper in my personal subjective and objective study of angels.

New creations ascend and descend

The Hebrew word for "angel" is "malak". According to the Strong's Concordance (#4397), "malak" can mean the following: ambassador, messenger, king, or angel. The word, malak, comes from a root word meaning: "to dispatch as a deputy; a messenger; specifically, of God".

2 Corinthians 5:16-20 (YLT)

¹⁶ <u>So that we henceforth have known no one according to the flesh</u>, and even if we have known Christ according to the flesh, yet now we know him no more;

¹⁷ so that if any one [is] in Christ -- [he is] a **new creature**; the old things did pass away, lo, become new have the all things.

¹⁸ And the all things [are] of God, who reconciled us to Himself through Jesus Christ, and did give to us the ministration of the reconciliation,

¹⁹ how that God was in Christ -- a world reconciling to Himself, not reckoning to them their trespasses; and having put in us the word of the reconciliation,

²⁰ in behalf of Christ, then, **we are ambassadors**, as if God were calling through us, we beseech, in behalf of Christ, `Be ye reconciled to God;'

It is these "**new creations**" (us) who are to be traveling to and from to God's presence. "New creations" are to be ascending and descending. In His presence we receive "the message" and then we are "dispatched as a deputies, as messengers, as **ambassadors**" to deliver the message with our words and lives! The trip is short since He abides in us.

If we do NOT TRAVEL, we have NO message!

According to the Greek New Testament concordance, the word "angelo" has been translated 150 of 176 occurrence as "angels". The conservative, frequent New Testament translation of the word "angelos" is the word "angel" not messenger, but we are not conservative – we are born from above; **we are sons of God**.

As messengers, one of our attributes is to travel, receive, deliver, and travel (repeat for additional pleasure). So it is NOT angels that travel but it is us (believing believers who believe) who travel.

> **John 3:3 (AMP)**
> ³ Jesus answered him, I assure you, most solemnly I tell you, that unless a person is born again (anew, from above), he cannot ever see (**know, be acquainted with, and experience**) the kingdom of God.

Traveling is equal to knowing, be acquainted with and experiencing the kingdom of God. I believe traveling is a mark of sonship.

All of creation is waiting for us to travel!

Creation Calls I

It was another Saturday night gathering and the worship was glorious. I closed my eyes to concentrate and listen to the path of worship. A few minutes into the worship set, in my mind's eye I saw a star. It was a lone star in a dark sky. I opened my eyes because the sight of star was distracting me from the worship.

I closed my eyes again and to my surprise, the star was still there. It seemed it was like that "burning bush that Moses turned aside to see". So since the star was still there - I began to "turn aside".

As I took a second look, the star came into focus. I perceived that the star was calling for "HELP!" I start to engage my mind to handle this unique unexpected request. But then reason started to intervene. With the intervention, unbelief began to resurrect.

I stopped thinking; I responded as a son.

With that decision, I began flying through outer space. The worship service was no longer real. Reality was now this rescue mission!

Flying from earth to this distant star - traveling NOT by understanding but traveling by obedience. Sons obey the call - a calling to deliver, secure, and free ALL creation.

I'm not sure how long or how far I traveled. But the star, it grew in size. As I approached the star, I also grew in size. **This was beyond my mind to comprehend but not my spirit.** It was as if, I needed to be a larger size to be the solution.

"We will be WHATEVER is needed for the situation!"

The star was "lacking an environment". So I breathed over the star and the star was refreshed. Then, I reached out and held the star in my hand. After a moment of gazing at the small star in my large hand, I placed the star into my being. Now, the star had an environment. I believe this was an example of glory made manifest.

I'm sure the Father could have saved the star Himself but it is a pleasing GLORY for a son to respond as a son. The right response always brings pleasure to the Father.

67

It seems it does not take long time OR a great effort to respond as son. When I returned, we were still in worship (and hopefully I had kept the right rhythm with my drum). In the next moment, someone went to the microphone to share a prophetic word. I wondered if I should share what I just experienced. As I thought about it, "leaving earth, traveling through space, talking stars..."

A son's appropriate response is pleasing to the Father

I could barely get my head around what I had experienced. As I thought about my encounter and the message from the pulpit, a verse dropped into me:

Jonah 1:17 (New International Version)
"Now the LORD provided a huge fish to swallow Jonah, and Jonah was in the belly of the fish three days and three nights."

I was surprised, that the verse in the book of Jonah actually supported my "star encounter". I received new revelations from this old story of Jonah and the big fish. The Lord could have "snagged" Jonah but He used a huge fish. Like providing the fish, the Lord has provided sons to HELP all creation BUT sons need to respond.

This huge fish was sent to swallow a human. This fish had never "swallowed" a human before. The fish did not know if it even had the capacity but it believed and obeyed. The huge fish obeyed and did the unnatural, swallowed Jonah. Unnatural can sometimes be supernatural.

The fish did something that was supernatural. A requirement to doing the supernatural is obedience; **thinking is NOT a requirement**. Reason is a hindrance to the miraculous.

Too much thinking can be a constraint to following His lead.

> In the kingdom, thinking can be a hindrance

I think if you want to participate in more Kingdom stuff like the huge fish and other sons, **you need to stop thinking yourself out of the invitations to the unknown and respond quickly!**

Creation Calls II

This encounter occurred about a year after my first 'stellar interaction' (Creation calling I). I had driven into Washington, DC to participate in an outdoor 24/7 worship event. I arrived for one of the night watches, found a spot near the front, set up my drum, and "jumped in the river". I've learned that worship is a "full contact sport". There are no benefits in spectating or watching the worship team.

> **Sons don't spectate**

This night I was pondering my King and a new concept, personal omnipresence. As the worship and pondering merged, I sensed a wind blowing around me. I initially thought I was entering a familiar encounter, the dance floor in my heart, but then I perceived that the swirling around me was something different. It seemed that the members of the Trinity were doing a circle dance around me. This was different and new experience. It was a bit 'unnerving' being the object of the Godhead's affections. It was hard trying to worship Them when They were giving me so much attention. As the dance continued, I believe I was being given the opportunity to realize that I was special and valuable. I was given a chance to be known; as They know me.

> I need to move from believing this to knowing this

Not sure when the circle dance ended, but I saw this chariot approach. As it came near, an arm reach out. The arm action seem to be an invitation to ride. This was not the way I had imagined Elijah's or others' chariot encounters. I stopped reasoning and grabbed the extended arm. Away we went - destination unknown.

The view was amazing. Space was brighter than I remembered. The Earth looked just like in the movies but brighter. I think, the driver paused to allow me to survey the scene. I know we were moving fast but I couldn't feel the speed. The next thing, I knew we landed on a space platform. I wasn't expecting, we were going to a platform. Anyway, I do enjoy a good adventure.

As I looked around, I wondered who made this platform. I heard in my mind that my FB friend, Jodi, had created this platform. Now I was confused because I couldn't validate the thought with a current memory. I couldn't recall if she had told me she had made a space platform or if I imagined that she had. I consider myself new at this stuff so I was not really aware that other people would be involved in my 'imaginary adventures'. I sensed that I was to contact her and thank her for building the platform. I gained a new appreciation for the scriptural truth, "...**every joint supplies**".

So folks, if you get prompted to create something don't think about it; JUST DO IT! There are consequences to your actions and your non-actions. I may not have landed if she had not responded as a son.

Anyway I was pondering my adventure and her cosmic construction. I was thoroughly distracted by my thoughts. When I looked up from my ponderings, there was a star standing in front of me. I'm not sure how long it had been 'standing' there or if it had been there before I landed.

Now I was really perplexed: "Why was a star on a space platform?"; "Why was I on a space platform?" Why, why,,,

---

Here's a rule of thumb: So in this realm or other realms, "If you are wondering something you should just ask"

The star said, *"I need you to breathe on me"*.

I thought, *"Why?"*

The star said, *"You've done it before."*

I could not recall, *"Ever breathing on a star..."*

All of sudden, *"I KNEW and I breathed on the star."*

The star went away.

Behind the star was a line of stars.

I don't remember a line of stars being there.

Why would there be a line of stars?

Now I knew the purpose of my journey.

I breathed on each star.

THE BREATH OF GOD IN YOU IS VALUABLE!

Romans 8:19-21 (AMP)
19 For [even the whole] creation <u>waits expectantly</u> and <u>longs earnestly for</u> God's sons to be made known [waits for the revealing, the disclosing of their sonship].

20 For the creation (nature) was subjected to a frailty (to futility, condemned to frustration), not because of some intentional fault on its part, but by the will of Him Who so subjected it—[yet] with the hope

*21 <u>That nature **(creation) itself will be set free**</u>from its bondage to decay and corruption [and gain an entrance] into the glorious freedom of God's children.*

When I returned, this thought bothered me, "How long had these stars been waiting for a son of God to show up?" I really believe "all creation" is very patient. But we should not take advantage of their patience.

They groan.

They wait.

They are frustrated. They ache.

We are their very present help in their time of need.

Their time for freedom **is now!**

72

Chapter 9 – Look Now Toward the Heavens

Genesis 15:5 Authorized Version (AV)
"And he brought him forth abroad, and said, *__Look now toward heaven__, and ¹tell the stars, if thou be able ²to number them: and he said unto him, So shall thy seed be."

The two words in the verse: (1) "tell"; "(2) "to number" – are the same Hebrew word, "**caphar**". At least, the word means to number or to score with a mark as a tally or record:

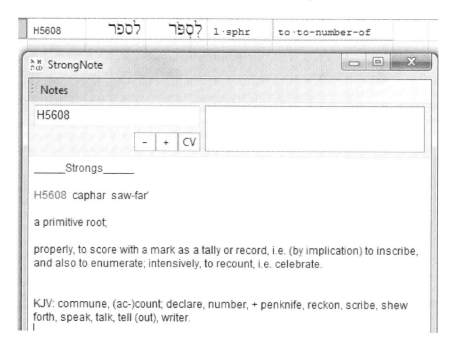

| H5608 | לִסְפֹּר | לִסְפֹּר | 1·sphr | to·to-number-of |

StrongNote

Notes

H5608

| – | + | CV |

_____Strongs_____

H5608 caphar saw-far'

a primitive root;

properly, to score with a mark as a tally or record, i.e. (by implication) to inscribe, and also to enumerate; intensively, to recount, i.e. celebrate.

KJV: commune, (ac-)count; declare, number, + penknife, reckon, scribe, shew forth, speak, talk, tell (out), writer.

When you look at the signs in the heavens, what is the message? It is a message of "ruling & dominion".

> When you **look to the heavens**, you are reminded that you are a ruler and you have dominion.

Relationship Dynamics

Let's look and learn from these interpersonal dynamics between our God and Abram. In order to do this, we should meditate on more of their relationship to glean a higher perspective of their union. Let's see more of their life in **Genesis chapter 15**:

> *¹ After these things, the word of the Lord came to Abram in a vision, saying, Fear not, Abram, I am your Shield, your abundant compensation, and your reward shall be exceedingly great.*
>
> *² And Abram said, Lord God, what can You give me, since I am going on [from this world] childless and he who shall be the owner and heir of my house is this [steward] Eliezer of Damascus?*
>
> *³ And Abram continued, Look, You have given me no child; and [a servant] born in my house is my heir.*
>
> *⁴ And behold, the word of the Lord came to him, saying, This man shall not be your heir, but he who shall come from your own body shall be your heir.*

Genesis 15 begins with a vision.

How do your times with the Father begin?

Let your engagement times begin with visions.

Raise your expectations. It is a **NEW** day.

Abram was known as a friend of God (James 2:23). If your goal is to become His friend, maybe we should take a second look. It is not a typical vision that we may be accustomed to. In this vision, Abram and God are having a disagreement. Yes, lovers sometimes disagree.

Amos 3:3 (KJV)
"Can two walk together, unless they be agreed?"

The answer to Amos 3:3 question is "No". So God had a creative way to bring the two into agreement. He would need Abram to see the situation from His perspective. Friends find a way.

Genesis 15:5
5 And He brought him outside [his tent into the starlight] and said, Look now toward the heavens and count the stars— if you are able to number them. Then He said to him, So shall your descendants be.

All relationships go through phases. If you press into your relationship with the Father; the bond will grow stronger. Abram believed in the Lord. Trust must be built. Trust is the foundation of a good, healthy relationship. Belief is the foundation of trust. Steadfast relationships are created as you pass through resistance and overcome dis-agreements.

Genesis 15:6 (AMP)

*⁶ And he [Abram] **believed in (trusted in, relied on, remained steadfast to) the Lord,** and He counted it to him as righteousness (right standing with God).*

Strong relationships are dynamic; passive relationships have no life. Notice also that as they overcame, Abram had a new revelation of the Lord, a new revelation of himself.

Genesis 15:7 (AMP)

⁷ And He said to him, I am the [same] Lord, Who brought you out of Ur of the Chaldees to give you this land as an inheritance.

Your true life is found in your dynamic relationship with God

Colossians 3:2 (AMP)

*"And **set** your **minds** and keep them **set** on what is above (the higher things), not on the things that are on the earth."*

It seems that this New Testament author had the same idea as God. He also had a revelation on how to obtain new life: "If you can get a person to take a <u>second look at the stars</u> ("what is above") then they will remember their first estate, their true life.

Colossians 3:1 (AMP)

If then you have been raised with Christ [to a new life, thus sharing His resurrection from the dead], aim at and seek the [rich, eternal treasures] that are above, where Christ is, seated at the right hand of God.

Sonship

YHVH sees from a High Place. So God brought Abraham outside of his tent into the starlight, into the heavens. There was more to this invitation than to just "count the stars" but to take a second look at the stars. God invited Abram back to man's first estate. Man's first estate is the role of a ruling king. Sons rule as kings.

> ### Psalm 147:4 (AMP)
> *He (God) determines and <u>counts the number of the stars</u>; He calls them all by their names.*

According to the above, it is the responsibility of YHVH to "count the stars". He even calls all the stars by name. Every creation with a name has a purpose. In the midst of YHVH's dynamic relationship with Abram, This is very similar to when YHVH brought the animals before Adam so that he would "name them". In any case, YHVH was sharing responsibility with His friend.

Counting the stars was reserved for Kings

YHVH It seems that friendship can lead to opportunities for responsibility and if you pass that test you become a son who can function as a king.

Kings command. Kings rule.   If you command and rule, so shall your seed command and rule. We all lead by example. Through His question, the Father implied, "If you establish this frequency – this will be true for your seed – to Abram's children and his children's children.

<u>This is a way that the Father works with a son.</u> As it was in the beginning, it is still true today, you are invited into a relationship with the Divine One.

77

Genesis 2:19 (AMP)

*"And out of the ground the Lord God formed every [wild] beast and living creature of the field and every bird of the air and brought them to **Adam** to see what he would call them; and whatever **Adam** called every living creature, that was its **name**."*

Again, this is a way that the Father works with His own. This is the relationship we were born for. The first Son, Jesus, says, "I only do what I see the Father doing". The Father demonstrates life to His sons, so we can imitate Him.

John 5:19 (AMP)

*So Jesus answered them by saying, I assure you, most solemnly I tell you, the Son is able to do nothing of Himself (of His own accord); but He is able to do only what He sees the Father doing, **for whatever the Father does is what the Son does in the same way [in His turn].***

This is the **LIFE** of sonship that Adam had. This is the **LIFE!** This is the **LIFE** of sonship Jesus lived and modelled. This **LIFE** is available to all who are born from above.

This is **LIFE**

This is **LIFE**; will you take the path of friendship which leads to responsibility and enter into the best **LIFE**?

This is so important I will repeat: "This is the way a Father works with a son." Jesus' earth time demonstrated how to be a son and how to relate to your heavenly Father. We have been given a new definition. This is the relationship simply stated in two sentences:

> ### John 5:20 (AMP)
> *The **Father** dearly loves the Son and disclosed to (shows) Him everything that He Himself does. And He will disclose to Him (let Him **see**) greater things yet than these, so that you may marvel and be full of wonder and astonishment.*

Jireh

There is another principle that I have discovered in YHVH. This principle was revealed in one of the names of YHVH, **YHVH Jireh**.

> ### Genesis 22:12-14 (YLT)
>
> [12] and He saith, `Put not forth thine hand unto the youth, nor do anything to him, for now I have known that thou art fearing God, and hast not withheld thy son, thine only one, from Me.'
>
> [13] And Abraham lifteth up his eyes, and looketh, and lo, a ram behind, seized in a thicket by its horns; and Abraham goeth, and taketh the ram, and causeth it to ascend for a burnt-offering instead of his son;

^{14} and Abraham calleth the name of that place `**Jehovah-Jireh**, because it is said this day in the mount, `Jehovah doth provide.'

A literal meaning of Jehovah-Jireh is "**The Lord who sees**", or The Lord Who Will See To It. "Jireh" is a H literally means "to see" or "to foresee". One of the benefits of having a friend, who is YHVH, is He has the ability to see and foresee. Note, a definition of the word "provide" is to make adequate preparation for a possible event. With those definitions, Jehovah-Jireh can fully mean: "**the Lord who will see to it that my every need is met**".

The One knows my need because **He sees**

Let us redefine the word, friend in this context of Jireh:
- A Friend who is able to meet my need in just the right time as He did for Abraham.
- A Friend who can meet my needs fully. In Abraham's dynamic relationship, it started with His Friend placing a ram in the thicket, a replacement offering for his son Isaac.

I think this is what we all long for: a personal, special Friend, One foresees our needs and also provides for those needs.

As can be seen in this dynamic relationship, "seeing" is tied to possession. Our birthright in His kingdom is sight. Perceiving is the birthright of everyone, who is born from above (John 3:3). Everyone who appropriately responds to YHVH is a candidate to experience the kingdom of God.

You can possess <u>whatever you perceive</u>

Conclusion

II Kings 23:5 (NKJ)
"Then he (King Josiah) removed the idolatrous priests whom the kings of Judah had ordained to burn incense on the high places in the cities of Judah and in the places all around Jerusalem, and those who burned incense to Baal, to the sun, to the moon, to the constellations, and to all the host of heaven."

We should take a clue from a fellow king, King Josiah. I caution the reader again NOT to *make the stars, the heavens, or the meanings of the Zodiac into idols.*

The stars which were strategically created and placed

These authors have explored many truths that are captured in the Mazzaroth. Here are a few excellent references:

1. "Mazzaroth" by Francis Rolleston 1862 Philologos Edition: Nov0901;
2. "The Gospel in the Stars" by Joseph A. Seiss;
3. "God's Voice in the Stars: Zodiac Signs and Bible Truth" by Ken Fleming;
4. "The Witness of the Stars" by E.W. Bullinger;
5. "The Heavens Declare: Jesus Christ Prophesied in the Stars" by William D. Banks;
6. "Mystery of the Mazzaroth: Prophecy in the Constellations" by Tim Warner;
7. **Christological Astronomy** can be found on Dr. Dale Sides website (www.lmci.org)

If you don't like reading, watch the 2014 movie, "*Interstellar*". It will give a new perspective of time, dimensions, stars, wormholes, humanity, black holes, and life.

Psalm 8 (AMP)

1 O Lord, our Lord, how excellent (majestic and glorious) is Your name in all the earth! You have set Your glory on [or above] the heavens.

2 Out of the mouths of babes and unweaned infants You have established strength because of Your foes, that You might silence the enemy and the avenger.

*3 **When I view and consider Your heavens, the work of Your fingers, the moon and the stars, which You have ordained and established,***

4 What is man that You are mindful of him, and the son of [earthborn] man that You care for him?

5 Yet You have made him but a little lower than God [or heavenly beings], and You have crowned him with glory and honor.

*6 **You made him to have dominion over the works of Your hands; You have put all things under his feet:***

7 All sheep and oxen, yes, and the beasts of the field,

8 The birds of the air, and the fish of the sea, and whatever passes along the paths of the seas.

9 O Lord, our Lord, how excellent (majestic and glorious) is Your name in all the earth!

I believe verses 3 and 6 of Psalm 8 are more than a great supporting scriptures. They are more than a nice verses that contains the word "star". **I believe those verses hold the key to understanding our true identity.** If you will "*view and consider the moon and the stars*" it will open a 'revelation portal' (dare I say a **star gate**) to the truth about your destiny.

Verse 6 is foundational truth for every mature son of God:

> "*You made him to have dominion over the works of Your hands; You have put all things under his feet*".

We were made to have dominion. He has put ALL things under our (mature) feet. If our potential is not as clear as a starry night, this great truth was restated again in the New Testament book of **Hebrews chapter 2:**

> [8] *For You have put everything in subjection under his feet.* ***Now in putting everything in subjection to man, He left nothing outside [of man's] control.*** *But at present we do not yet see all things subjected to him [man].*

We are **NOT** "yet seeing all things subjected to" us because we have **NOT** fully taken a second look at the stars!

NOW is the time to take a second look

Amos 5:8 (AMP)
[8] **Seek Him** Who made the cluster of stars called Pleiades and the constellation Orion... **the Lord is His name**.

SELAH

83

"Twinkle, twinkle, little star,
Now I know what you are.
Up above the world so high,
Communicating messages in the sky.

Twinkle, twinkle, little star,
Now I know what you are.
Created for a purpose so diverse,
Now we can team to change the multi-verse.

Maker of the stars,
You are beautiful by far.
Creator of all above,
Thank you for your lavish love."

- Author Known Very Well

In conclusion, our Awesome Creative God has provided the message of glory. The message is written in the heavens and in the bible. There are a multitude of benefits for anyone who will take a second look at the stars.

Your destiny is in the twinkle.

More resources for your journey:

1. *www.newmystic.net*

2. *www.new-mystic.podomatic.com*

Appendix: Christological Astronomy Profile

www.christologicalastronomy.com, the Christological Astronomy website was designed to help you understand and help reveal to you what God has wanted you to know. This message has been available for you before you were born.

This is not astrology; rather it will support the claims that astrology has attempted to counterfeit astronomy and cloaked glorious truths.

A sovereign and omniscient God created both people and the heavens and the Scriptures say that He called us out before the foundation of the world (Ephesians 1:4). He predetermined our birth dates and providentially arranged the sun, moon, and planets to announce our callings and gifts. He provides the advantage so we can be victorious during every day of our lives.

I was shocked and amazed of how insightful and edifying this report was for me. Like receiving in prophetic word, you need to test it. The report identified insights into my predestinated calling, gifts, and purposes according to the celestial Word of God. The celestial word of God which supplements the written and spoken word of God. I'm still amazed.

I guess this report could be my biography since it is absolutely true. So get to know more about me and then get your own report. This is a Level One report. There are additional reports that provide greater prophetic insight for you. **When you know you were destined to be significant; you will live significantly.**

It is quite the story how I received this report. Even a bigger story of how I received twelve hours of **Christian Astronomy** teaching from Dr. Dale Sides before publishing this book.

My Level 1 Christological Astronomy Profile Summary

Planet	Constellation
The Sun	Taurus
Mercury	Taurus
Venus	Taurus
Mars	Pisces
Ceres	Taurus
Jupiter	Aquarius
Saturn	Capricorn

My Christological Astronomy Profile Report

Birthday: Thursday May 17, 1962

****

The Sun

The location of the Sun is the most contributing factor in interpreting a Christological profile. The Sun is the only light in the solar system that has light of itself. Jesus referred to Himself as "the light of the world" in John 8:12 and 9:5. All other celestial bodies reflect the light of the Sun. The constellation that the Sun was in at the time of your birth shows certain traits and messianic characteristics that are potential within you. (Remember that the Sun's location is not the same as in horoscopes and astrology, due to precession.)

The Sun is a picture of Yeshua the Righteous One. Even though the righteousness of God is a gift and not to be earned, the location of the Sun will show your "righteous acts." These are the rewards that you will accrue in your earthly visitation. In other words, when God says, "Well done good and faithful servant," it will be a stamp of approval for fulfilling what the Sun said about you in your birth sky.

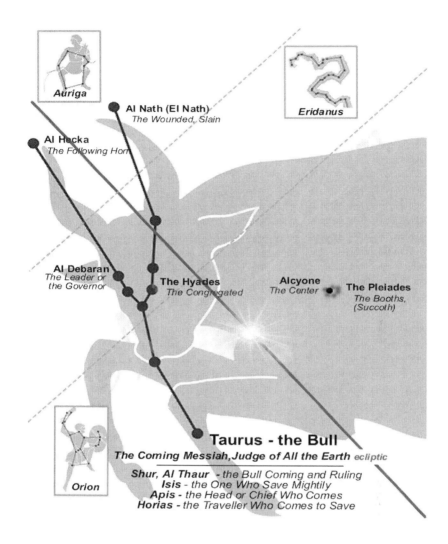

Auriga

Al Nath (El Nath)
The Wounded, Slain

Eridanus

Al Hecka
The Following Horn

Al Debaran
*The Leader or
the Governor*

The Hyades
The Congregated

Alcyone
The Center

The Pleiades
*The Booths,
(Succoth)*

Orion

Taurus - the Bull
The Coming Messiah, Judge of All the Earth ecliptic

Shur, Al Thaur - *the Bull Coming and Ruling*
Isis - *the One Who Save Mightily*
Apis - *the Head or Chief Who Comes*
Horias - *the Traveller Who Comes to Save*

Meaning

Level One

- ⑩ The Sun, the most dominant image of the heavens, resides in Taurus, the raging bull.
- ⑩ Taurus shows the Lord returning in judgment with focused determination.
- ⑩ The means you were called to have strong convictions and opinions.

The Sun in Taurus is the bold announcement of the Lord coming in judgment with determination and fervor. This is the first part of the last trilogy of the ages: His first coming (Virgo–Sagittarius); the time from Pentecost till now (Capricorn–Aries), and the future of His second coming (Taurus–Leo). This shows the tenacity and bullishness of the coming King. He will not be denied. This portrays the coming Judge with His mind made up.

****

Mercury

The planet Mercury was named after the Roman god who was a messenger. The Hebrew name for this planet is *Kovah Chammah*, meaning "the Sun's messenger." Mercury always travels close to the Sun, and the location of Mercury in your birth sky will show the messianic message that you can carry and champion.

Meaning

Level One

- ⑩ Mercury, the messenger planet, resides in Taurus, the raging bull.
- ⑩ Taurus shows the Lord returning in judgment with focused determination.
- ⑩ This means you were called to have a strong voice and strong convictions and opinions.

Mercury, the messenger planet, residing in Taurus shows a strong word to be delivered. This is not someone who dances around issues but is forthright and bold. You are called to deliver a bold word. Don't be intimated by the criticisms of others. It is who you are.

****

Venus

Venus' Hebrew name is *Nogah*, which means "bright" and "splendorous." The Roman name was given to this planet to honor their goddess of beauty and passion. In this sense, the mythological name still carries the messianic message of passion and love. The messianic message of Venus is very simple—the love of Christ.

Meaning

Level One

- ⑩ Venus, the planet of passion and love, is located in Taurus, the raging bull.
- ⑩ Taurus shows the Lord returning in judgment with focused determination.
- ⑩ This means you are passionate about your beliefs. You are opinionated.

Venus, the passionate one, residing in Taurus, the determined one, shows you are passionate about your ideas and want to share them with everyone. You zeal is communicable and enthusiastic.

****

Mars

Mars' Hebrew name is *Madim*, meaning "red." It is the red planet and red represents fervor—what you will fight for, bleed for, and potentially what you will die for. The messianic message of Mars is this aspect of "Yeshua the Warrior" being manifested through you.

Meaning

Level One

- ⑩ Mars, the red planet of fervor and zeal, is positioned in Pisces, the two fishes.
- ⑩ Pisces, the two fishes, shows abundance of relationships; both with God and other people.
- ⑩ This shows the relationship you will fight for: if Mars is in the vertical band, you will fight for your relationship and time with God; if it is in the horizontal fish, it shows you are willing to fight to maintain relationships with people.

Mars, the warrior planet, residing in Pisces, the relational constellation, shows where and for whom you are willing to fight. If Mars is in the vertical band, it shows a fervor and desire to defend the name of God and to fight for His rights of recognition and worship. In the horizontal band, it shows vehemence for people and fighting for them. In level 2 you can learn how to find the exact location of Mars.

Ceres

Ceres is the largest of the asteroids orbiting around the Sun between Mars and Jupiter. Everyone agrees that at one time it was a planet. (There will be more about this in level 2 and level 3.) We again are dealing with astronomy and not astrology. Ceres, of all the planets, holds a mystique about it—mainly, what caused it to explode. The Hebrew name is *Rahab* and it is mentioned by name in two separate places in the Bible (Psalm 89:10 and Isaiah 51:9). The location of Rahab, or Ceres, in your profile shows the possible places of attack or weaknesses. Hence, it shows what you need to study and guard against—areas commonly attacked, possible strongholds of pride, or even potential blind spots.

Focusing on Ceres is one of the issues of the levels 2 and 3.

Meaning

Level One

Ceres is a small planetoid that revolves round the Sun between Mars and Jupiter. It is the largest of a belt of asteroids that most astronomers believe was previously a planet before it exploded or was bombed by another asteroid. Much to the surprise of many, it is mentioned in the Bible (e.g., Isaiah 52:19 and Psalm 89:10) and is called Rahab or Rakab. This is a *major* piece of the whole puzzle when reading planets and locations. Our computer program's accuracy has NASA reconsidering its ephemerides. Its location and meaning requires more explanation and is given at level 2 along with the interpretations of Uranus and Neptune.

Jupiter

Jupiter is the head god of the pantheon of Rome; his name was Zeus to the Greeks. The planet Jupiter is the largest planet by far and namesake-wise, it holds a regal position even among the other planets. It shows the leadership and courage of Yeshua.

Meaning

Level One

- ⑩ Jupiter, the leadership planet, is situated in Aquarius, the water bearer.
- ⑩ Aquarius has a water urn pouring out of his belly; this shows the Christological aspect of being an abundant giver.
- ⑩ You are blessed and highly favored. Freely you have received; freely give, and lead others in the cause of giving. Giving is one of the great manifestations of godliness. Be an example of giving. This also can relate to being fervent for the gifts of the Holy Spirit.

The king planet, Jupiter, residing in Aquarius, the blessings outpoured, declares that you are called to lead a charge to renew relationships and the power of the Holy Spirit. Aquarius is about blessings being poured out; Jupiter shows the kingly messianic leadership. This is where you are supposed to lead, perhaps among other things as well.

****

Saturn

Saturn's ancient, mystical Hebrew name of *Shabbat* helps in identifying the Christology of this, the seventh planet from the Sun. Interestingly, the root word of *Shabbat* means the "Sabbath"—the seventh day of the week. Saturn with all its glorious rings and beauty shows the consummate messianic contribution of your life in faithfulness and service. This is the hill to die on!

Meaning

Level One

- ⑩ Saturn, the seventh planet of faithfulness and service, is in Capricorn, the sacrifice.
- ⑩ Capricorn, the dying goat and living fish, shows being sacrificial to help others overcome.
- ⑩ You have strength to persevere in selflessness. Mercy is a trait you admire and have.

Saturn, the seventh planet from the Sun, residing in Capricorn, the sacrificial redeemer, shows the maturity level of service. This shows an endurance level of service to the needy. Whether Saturn is in the first or latter part of Capricorn makes a lot of difference in the goat/fish interpretation.

Level 2 will take you into deeper Christological interpretations of your birth sky by considering the unseen planets of Ceres, Uranus, and Neptune. These interpretations show your potential; but it will be your diligence and persistence in these areas that will help you build these Christ-like characteristics and bring that potential into reality.

+++++++

❿ Planet: The Sun

The location of the Sun is the most contributing factor in interpreting a Christological profile. The Sun is the only light in the solar system that has light of itself. Jesus referred to Himself as "the light of the world" in John 8:12 and 9:5. All other celestial bodies reflect the light of the Sun. The constellation that the Sun was in at the time of your birth shows certain traits and messianic characteristics that are potential within you. (Remember that the Sun's location is not the same as in horoscopes and astrology, due to precession.)

The Sun is a picture of Yeshua the Righteous One. Even though the righteousness of God is a gift and not to be earned, the location of the Sun will show your "righteous acts." These are the rewards that you will accrue in your earthly visitation. In other words, when God says, "Well done good and faithful servant," it will be a stamp of approval for fulfilling what the Sun said about you in your birth sky.

🔟 Constellation: Taurus

Taurus (the bull) - He is the blood of the bull, as a profile of Old Testament offerings for redemption.

Coming Messiah
Judge of All Earth
Charging bull
Great determination and strong will
Purpose driven
Dedicated to finishing the fight
Protective of others

Decans:
Orion—conqueror
Eridanus—river of the judge
Auriga—shepherd protecting his people

Taurus is the figure of a charging bull, indicative of *great determination* and a *strong will*. This kind of determination was demonstrated christologically by His dedication to finish the fight at Calvary. These stand strong in the Lord (Ephesians 6:10).

47644521R00053

Made in the USA
Charleston, SC
16 October 2015